A Chinese Ouroboros

Ryan Shen

BookLeaf Publishing

India | USA | UK

Presentation by *BookLeaf Publishing*

Web: www.bookleafpub.com

E-mail: info@bookleafpub.com

ISBN: 9789360942243

First edition 2024

For those who have chosen to read a copy of this book, I hope I bring about inspiration to also manifest what you want in your life as well.

PREFACE

This book threads together a few things I grew up learning both in school and at home, as well as making references to specific parts of pop culture that my inner child loves.

At home, I had learned to solve math problems earlier than my peers because of my father, and that gave me an opportunity to stand out within the classroom and that made me like math. As a result I paid more attention to numbers. Because this book touches on mythological and magical symbolism, it is natural that I then pay attention to the number of things. There are 19 poems, which is a prime number. The number twelve is part of a cosmic order in traditions from Greek mythology, Chinese Zodiac signs, and even in the Old Testament, and I showcase that here.

Aside from Old World references, this is a celebration of what has made it into the mainstream narrative that stand outside of the cultural norms today. There are several film references, gay and trans, and speculative. Some references may be hidden from the reader, but to find a way to plant them into my work is key in keeping me motivated in creative writing.

Clownish Path to Pride

Comforted by the stay in the womb, my parents expected a boy. Oh void, why did you forsake me and not take me? Instead, you took my emotions and left me with sadness. What script was I to follow to avoid disappointment!

A strange mime waved to me and boarded me on a train, leaving this little town and heading to a wicked other little town. Clowns hugged me and I felt welcomed. No one cared that I was a little strange.

My troupe would be embraced by applause on stage. And they would groom themselves to draw attention even if it were actually a cage. Dancing like peacocks in heat, they made the spectators bring down a green flurry!

Banning!
Banning!
Banning!

One day, I was cawed to join, and brought colors that stood out as a peahen like no other. I grew tail feathers bigger than all the cages they used to contain us.

And since, brought food for us so that no hunger remained!

A Human Unbecoming

I cut myself a profound wound.

It altered my soul, becoming tasked to take
What belonged to others
With every throbbing,
Fluids flowed
Plastering every surface
Pounding every crevice
Until my body was wasted.

Acidic sand replaced organic basic,
And my body became part of the land,
While my soul at the gates was remanded.

Transcendental Crossings

Unblinkingly, I stared at the sky until stars
twinkled and dust clouded my eyes.
Holding stillness with such conviction, it was
like my metabolism was under incantation.

The grass grew rapidly and boldly around me,
after the rain and nourishing sunshine.
I thought myself to be a blade of grass among
many...

until you stepped on me.

I awoke to the pain you inflicted,
And found that we both spoke English.
We agreed for you to nurse the wounds formed
by the impact of your feet.
In time my obstruction to your path became a
blessing...

Both you and I

Life-Changing Sands

Your gaze...
Your questions...
Your reassurance of interest...

What you did
Convinced the child within of a true witness.
Equal in naivety and curiosity,
We became each other's co-pilot.

You held onto my thigh while using the steering wheel,
On the way to the beach with a bucket in my hand.

A builder's project became a well.
In the depths of digging, the water's beckoned
Called me to drink and join in hell

In fury's grip, your scowl adorned,
Yet, as I changed hues, a frown was born.
Into the well's abyss, you swiftly dove,
Caught me in descent, a testament of love.

Hidden skills, extraordinary and rare,
Revealed in that moment of a whispering prayer.

Trio of Haikus

6

At the edge of death
I received from Basquiat's tomb
Renewed mission

The source gifted me
A new life within my womb
I had not removed

Welcomed miracle
For you were most nurturing
I welled up with pride

A Generative Anger

7

Black goddesses gave me euphoria of the mind and
I became a willing missionary.

I prepared a feast to strengthen our friends to break more shackles.
My friends advertised a public rager that conjured that
Crown Victoria with a megaphone shouting,
"Is there trouble here?"

It was so loud it shook my grounds but my friends held me down.

Wallowing in fertile mud together,
covering the yellow on my belly,
I became pregnant.
This child, most rebellious yet
whispers to me,
"Keep us safe."
A spell was cast in a moment,
in a movement.

Let it be known: I am not alone.

A greater force is at work.

A Fatherhood Celebration

Tiny fingers, a grasp so small,
A precious heartbeat within the squall.
Eyes that mirror the morning light,
A father's joy takes its first flight.

A mirror reflecting hopes and dreams,
Yet, not immune to life's extremes.
Heartaches woven in the tapestry,
Of parenthood's complex mystery.

Release the burdens, let forgiveness flow,
In the fertile soil, new seeds to sow.
Embrace the innocence, reclaim the play,
Let laughter echo, brighten the day.

Each stumble and each tender smile,
A growing bond that spans a mile.
With every tear and laughter's ring,
Brings up a complex set of feelings.

A Motherly Resolution

In a world where capitalism holds its sway,
I'm torn from my motherland, a price to pay.
Colonists' currency, a twisted invention,
For a bag of rice, I make the concession.

Contaminated waters, a bitter brew,
To feed my baby, in hardships we strew.
To persevere, adapt, collect in their coin,
In colonial echoes, my dreams embroil.

Lineage must persist, though the cost is steep,
In colonial currency, my wages reap.
Shortening my days, my sacrifice profound,
For the future of my kin, on this foreign ground.

Bitterness swallowed, an enduring taste,
As they live decades, a contrasting haste.
Frugal, hard work, a relentless chore,
For in my child's prosperity, I find my core.

Through the currents of time, our spirits strive,
Bring us a future where all our children thrive!
Bring us a future where all our children thrive!

Separate Togetherness

Our babies were clearly confused
They heard our voices together, even though
We were apart

You tried to act naturally
But they kept trying to reach for me
Struggling to hold it together, they spilt milk onto the phone

The accident was a deafening silence
I could not withhold my tears
For who knew when I would hear from you or them again?

Was maintaining a long distance connection cruel kindness?
Late at night, I stayed awake
Worrying, was there not enough goodwill between us?

As the sun rose, I felt like the living dead
My hands reached and eyes read through your e-mail
"Let's watch Wong Kar-Wai together"

Who is the wiser fool?
I romantically imagined you besides me in bed
A marathon of films to find the moon beautiful again

// Days of Being Dystopically Queer //

// In the Mood For Love //

Behind my playful cool
Lingers an ache that makes me
Scream secrets in trees

// 2046 //

Holidays spent in alternative universes
Cannot substitute my true poetic pal
I will not settle for a knockoff chorus

// Happy Together //

Even though we aren't meant to be
I still love you
And wish we could've seen the waterfall
together

A Fantastic Mortal Sin

12

Not immortal unfortunately,
I must travel to the antipode
For the elixir of life

Who knew that I would meet a tall glass of water?
I quenched my thirst for wildness and longevity
Living an equivalent Brokeback mountain life
I could not quit

My postcard boomeranged with a stamp
Marking your tragic demise
And your name Lan Yu became one I used to author

Twelve

In the cosmic tapestry, where destinies align,
Each soul to tribes of twelve, the stars assign.
Separated by the Zodiac's celestial grace,
A vow cast when oceans embraced space.

As the Holy land split, a cosmic decree,
Oceans spread wide, a vast, tumultuous sea.
I pledged to tame sea monsters, wild and untamed,
Dreaming of ruling, where Neptune's realm was named.

I sought for you but you did not want to be found.
You were able and became time unbound.

The flames from the sun dried up all the oceans.
Alone I cried a river of tears, with no more motions.

But Earth was in dire need of you, savior,
From reckless inconsiderate human behavior.

Four elements in anticipation stand,
Awaiting your being, supreme and grand.
With your light, destructive forces ceased,
Life flourished, alliances formed in peace.

Rats, dragons, and monkeys head northward bound,
Oxen, snakes, and roosters to the west were found.
Tigers, horses, and dogs to the southern shores,
Rabbits, goats, and pigs to the east, where life restored.

Abraham

Since God sowed the seeds with the melody of
"This Land is Mine," a kingdom in your heart
did shine. With a tilt toward optimistic dreams,
you yearned to mold reality's streams. Yet, in
passive hopes and wishes spun, you grew
disgruntled under the sun.

Fertile soil, fertile beings, the desire profound,
In frustration, you left the known ground.
Convincing a following with a melodic plea,
"Follow, follow, follow," to the redwood sea.

But your journey's end, in Salt Lake's embrace,
A campfire's glow, a prophet misplaced.
The redwoods' whispers lost in the city's hum,
A false prophecy, where dreams succumb.

Wanda

To grieve the life you didn't have,
You created new lives for yourself
Based on characters in your childhood TV shows

You wiggled your nose
Like it was tickled by a feather duster
Calculated a path to traverse with your fingers
Then started to fight off opposing officers

As the clay pot
Split and spilled
Branded you with a scarlet letter
You lost the Schrödinger space
Where your children lingered

Deirdre

We were taxed and tired
Carrying all the weight on our shoulders
We had to do everything,
Make our own love to be loveable

Their relentless pursuit
Transformed me into a canary in a coal mine
With my vest bright and yellow
Made your eyes hungry for mine

All at once inspired to sing
You huffed but puffed
Until our hiding place was covered in dust
And you fell through the cracks of this world to
another

A Laborious Epic

In the gig economy's rhythm,
You found your start,
A dogwalker's tale, a journey, a part.
Hired by a farmer with pens of lore,
Erymanthian pigs, chaos galore.
Golden-horned goats with ancient might,
Oxen from Crete, a presence in the night.
Mares that tasted Diomedes' grim feast,
Angry birds with metal beaks, hung deceased.

With Bingo, my companion in this dance,
King Eury whispered secrets, a mysterious
trance.
Cerberus, the dog, in disguise concealed,
For flying monkeys, fate soon revealed.

An extra tip lured me on a quest,
To cleanse rat-infested pens, an earnest test.
Upon tiger-printed sheets, secrets shared,
A regular on Taskrabbit, destiny paired.

Unexpectedly, the farmer's demand,
Drained my wages, a treacherous hand.
Retribution's choice, a girdle's swift theft,
Powers bestowed, a destiny deft.

Encounters with creatures, wild and free,
Conversations with a snake, a mystery.
A dragon convinced with words so skilled,
To orchards it ventured, apple-picking thrilled.

Hesperides' apples, knowledge they shared,
Cloak lifted, truths revealed, destiny dared.
The brick road unfolded, Eden's view,
In the gig economy's journey, a poetic hue.

Eastern Odyssey

I travelled from the river to the sea
Ocean to ocean, until I reached Mount Fuji

Eating apples you waxed
My desire of flesh waned

Ascending on relationship gondolas
Sliding down dopamine lanes

Was I a human or a caterpillar?
I ponder as I wake
A butterfly from a cocoon-break

With a renewed life force
I tasted nectar from your flower
In a garden next to Lao Tian Ye's tower
This will be my home for all of my hours

A Capybara's Ode

If you are bright-eyed and bushy-tailed,
I accept whatever you discover
Through your windows, we learn together.

If you dare, we'll ride an alligator together
Or tell me, "not for a while crocodile."
Or whatever thing to get me to smile.

If you are overwhelmed, close your eyes.
Even with your mask, I know your true stripes,
For you have managed all of the gripes.

If you are hungry, we'll eat bamboo together,
Till you are sleepy or need to hide from the
elements, Our foxhole will keep us safe
whatever the developments.

Cycles

A free-spirited pair exploring together
Floated down a well, a rabbit-hole discovered.

Following arrows and strange trail markers,
They joined a banquet with a suited crocodile.

Consuming "Drink Me" potions and "Eat Me"
cake, Sense of selves lost as their tails did shake.

This ringleader brought upon a change profound,
Human forms by his command were bound.

Sold to a circus for performance purpose,
Jumping across flames on bamboo bikes,
A destiny altered, an affair unfair.

Then came a faithful smoky night,
A figure eight path shifted ever so slight.
They made for a break as death they both faked.